A Note to Parents

DK READERS is a compelling program for beginning readers, designed in conjunction with leading literacy experts, including Dr. Linda Gambrell, Director of the Eugene T. Moore School of Education at Clemson University. Dr. Gambrell has served on the Board of Directors of the International Reading Association and as President of the National Reading Conference.

Beautiful illustrations and superb full-color photographs combine with engaging, easy-to-read stories to offer a fresh approach to each subject in the series. Each DK READER is guaranteed to capture a child's interest while developing his or her reading skills, general knowledge, and love of reading.

The five levels of DK READERS are ⸢ᵉrent reading abilities, enabling you to choos⸍ ⸍at are exactly right for your child:

Pre-level 1: Learning to read
Level 1: Beginning to read
Level 2: Beginning to read alone
Level 3: Reading alone
Level 4: Proficient readers

The "normal" age at which a child begins to read can be anywhere from three to eight years old, so these levels are only a general guideline.

No matter which level you select, you can be sure that you are helping your child learn to read, then read to learn!

LONDON, NEW YORK, MUNICH,
MELBOURNE, and DELHI

Series Editor Deborah Lock
Designer Sadie Thomas
U.S. Editor Elizabeth Hester
Production Alison Lenane
DTP Designer Almudena Díaz
Jacket Designer Simon Oon

Reading Consultant
Linda Gambrell, Ph.D.

First American Edition, 2004
13 14 13 12 11 10
Published in the United States by DK Publishing, Inc.
345 Hudson Street, New York, New York 10014
013-DD204-Oct/2004
Copyright © 2004 Dorling Kindersley Limited

Published in Great Britain by Dorling Kindersley Limited

Library of Congress Cataloging-in-Publication Data
In the park.-- 1st American ed.
    p. cm. -- (DK readers, pre-level 1)
    ISBN 978-0-7566-0535-3 (hbk)   978-0-7566-0537-7 (pbk)
    1. Parks--Juvenile literature. 2. Parks--Recreational use--Juvenile
literature. I. Dorling Kindersley readers. Pre-level 1, Learning to read.
    SB481.3.I52 2004
    363.6'8--dc22
                                              2004007459

Color reproduction by Colourscan, Singapore
Printed and bound in the U.S.A. by Lake Book Manufacturing, Inc.

The publisher would like to thank the following for their kind
permission to reproduce their photographs:
a=above; c=center; b=below; l=left; r=right t=top;
7 Corbis: Jon Feingersh. **8 Photolibrary.com:** Warwick Kent tl. **10–11
Corbis:** Larry Williams. **10 DK Picture Library:** Stephen Oliver.**12–13
Alamy Images:** Lynn Freeny. **12 Getty Images:** Darrell Gulin tl. **12 DK
Picture Library:** Barrie Watts. **14 DK Picture Library:** Stephen Oliver.
16–17 DK Picture Library: John Bulmer. **18 Corbis:** Ariel Skelley. **21
Photolibrary.com. 22–23 Powerstock:** Martin Rugner. **23 DK Picture
Library:** Royal Signals Museum, Blandford Camp. **24–25 Getty Images:**
Photodisc Blue. **25 DK Picture Library:** Barnabas Kindersley. **26 Corbis:**
Sygma. **28–29 Alamy Images:** Steve Popichak. **29 Corbis:** Richard
Cummins tr. **30–31 Zefa Visual Media.**

All other images © Dorling Kindersley
For further information see: www.dkimages.com

Discover more at
www.dk.com

DK **READERS**

LEARNING
pre-level
1
TO READ

In the Park

DK Publishing, Inc.

We like going
to the park.

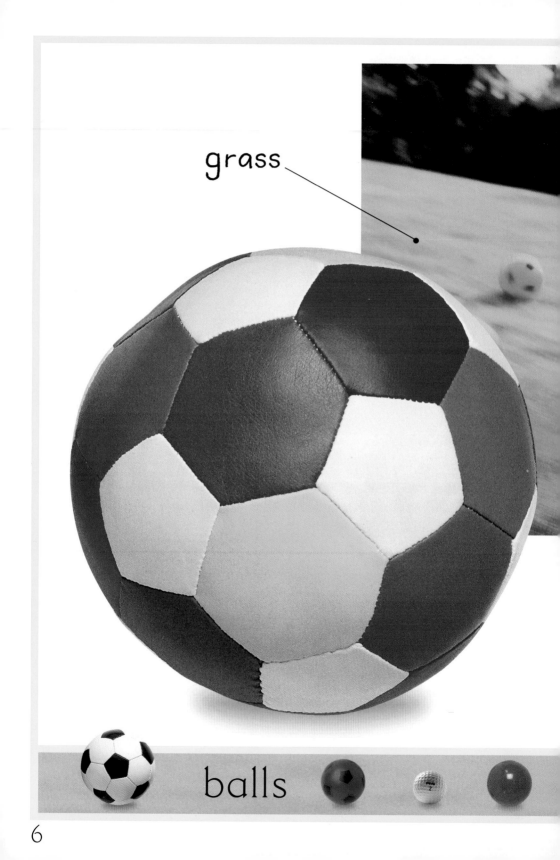

grass

balls

We kick the ball
across the grass.

string

bow

kites

We fly kites
in the sky.

bat————•

We play baseball
with bats
and balls.

 baseball

ball

We watch ducks
on the pond.

 ducks

pond

feathers

13

water

We sail boats
on the water.

boats

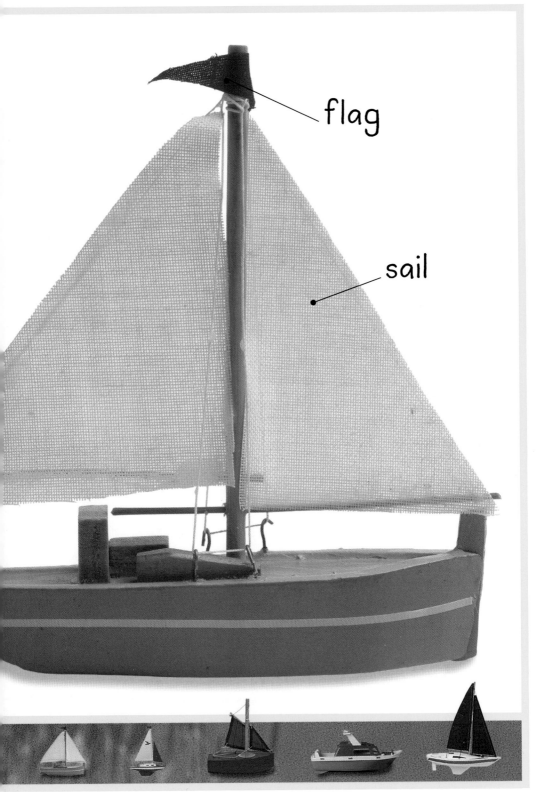

flag

sail

15

rope

jungle gyms

We climb on the jungle gym.

slide

swings

We play
on the swings.

feet

seat

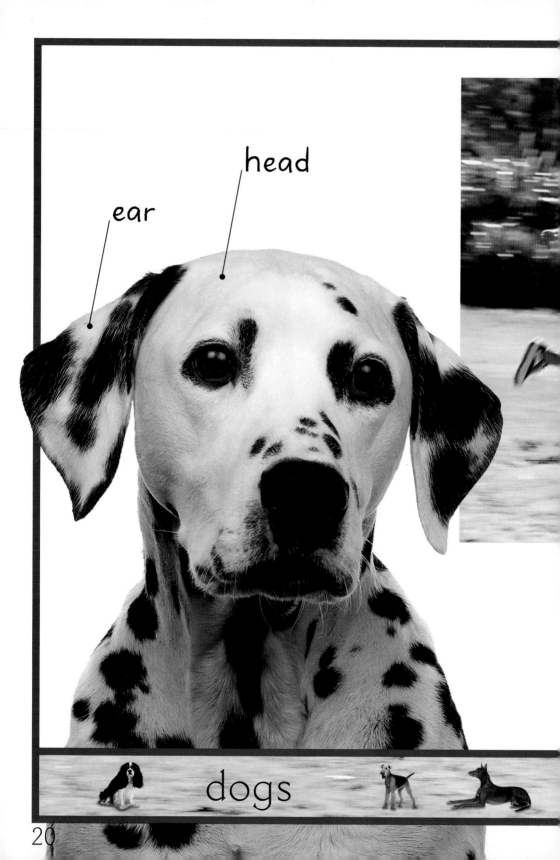

head

ear

dogs

We run and run
with our dogs.

We ride our bicycles
through the grass.

 bicycles

handlebar

pedal

wheel

helmet

in-line skates

We roll along on our in-line skates.

wheel

We play a game
of hide-and-seek.

 hide-and-seek

hand

nut

fur

squirrels

We watch the squirrels gather nuts.

What do you like

The park is
lots of fun!

roundabout

to do best?

Picture word list

ball
page 6

kite
page 8

baseball
page 10

duck
page 12

boat
page 14

jungle gym
page 16

swing
page 18

dog
page 20

bicycle
page 22

in-line skate
page 24

hide-and-seek
page 26

squirrel
page 28